Better Homes and Gardens
TRADEMARK

CHRISTMAS DECORATIONS

CHILDREN CAN MAKE

TREASURE PRESS

Christmas Decorations Children can Make
Crafts Editor: Sara Jane Treinen,
    Elizabeth Porter
Editorial Project Manager: James D. Blume
Graphic Designers: Linda Ford Vermie,
    Harijs Priekulis
Electronic Text Processor: Paula Forest

This edition first published in Great Britain in 1989 by:
Treasure Press
Michelin House
81 Fulham Road
London SW3 6RB

Original edition published by Meredith Corporation in the
United States of America.

BETTER HOMES AND GARDENS is a registered trademark in
Canada, New Zealand, South Africa, and other countries.

ISBN 1-85051-386-4

Produced by Mandarin Offset
Printed in Hong Kong

CONTENTS

Parade Into Christmas

Let these high-stepping soldiers march across a mantle of greenery to announce the holiday season at your house. Why not make one for your music teacher? It's a perfect gift and one you can make all by yourself.

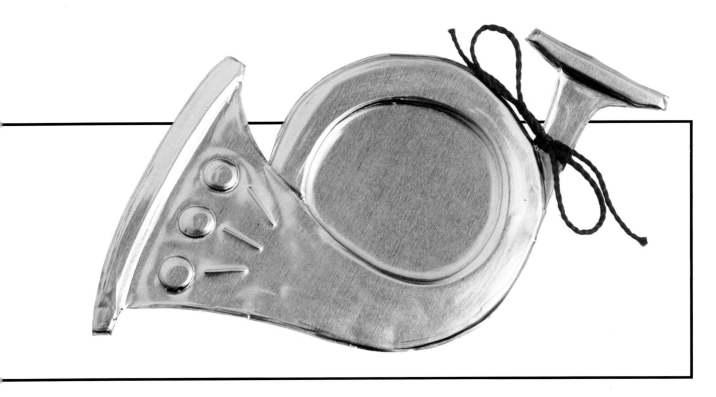

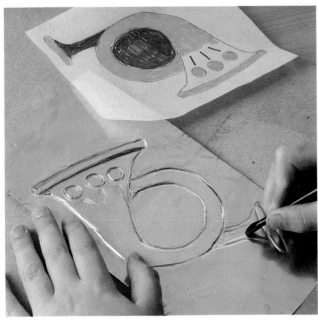

4 Turn the foil so the gold side is up. With the orange stick, push down all of the areas of the foil that are coloured red on the pattern.

5 Cut out the design. Smooth any bends or rough edges with the orange stick.

6 Tie a 26cm piece of red string in a bow around the neck of the horn.

Make the tin foil soldiers from the silver side of the aluminium foil following steps 1–5. Then colour the soldiers with the felt-tip pens.

Tin Foil Soldiers and Brass Horns

_____ Retrace the blue lines
on the back side

████ Rub the red areas
on the front side

Rub the yellow areas
on the back side

Make paper soldiers...

Trace the soldier patterns on to thick
paper or thin card. Colour the soldiers
with crayons or felt-tip pens. Cut out the
shapes. Use them as ornaments for your
tree or to decorate a present, as shown
on pages 30–35.

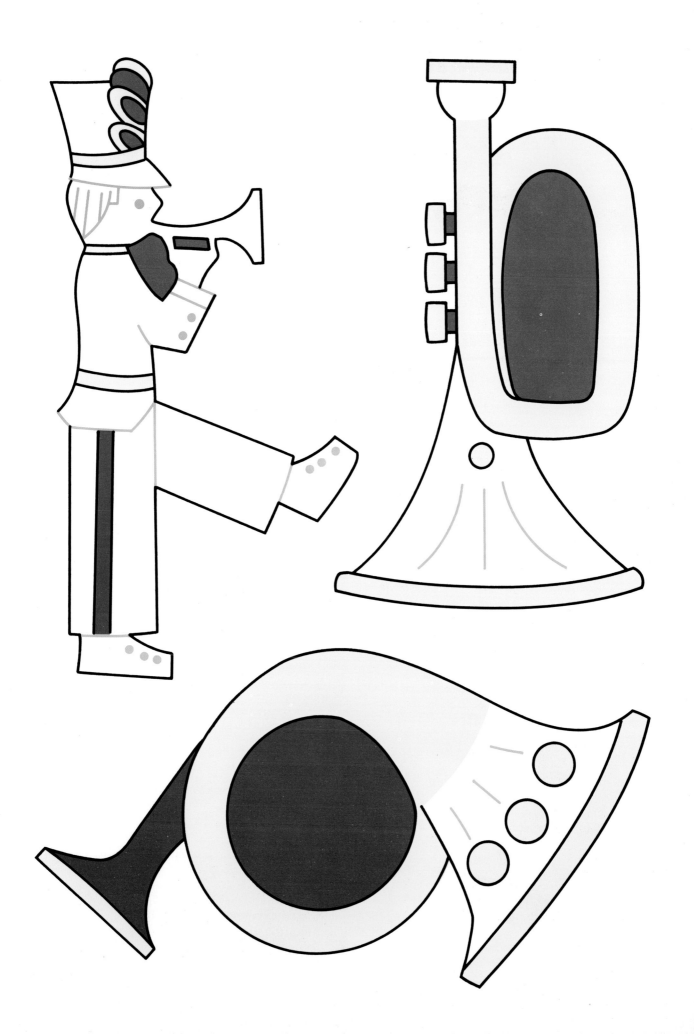

Make Your Own Cards

Lots of people—teachers, grandmas and grandpas, even brothers and sisters—would love to receive a Christmas card that you made all by yourself. For a special touch, write your own holiday wishes on the inside of the card.

Marbleized Cards

Cut out holiday shapes from bright-coloured marbleized paper
to make your own cards and gift tags.

Materials you will need...

- ☐ Heavy, white watercolour paper
- ☐ Oil-based paints
- ☐ 22 x 33cm tin
- ☐ Aluminium foil
- ☐ Drinking glass
- ☐ Paper towels
- ☐ Toothpicks
- ☐ Tweezers or tongs
- ☐ Tracing paper
- ☐ Scissors
- ☐ Hole puncher
- ☐ Pencil

1 Line the tin with aluminium foil. Fill the tin with about 5cm of water. Place the glass near the tin. Place paper towels under and all around the glass.

2 Stir the paint in the jar with a toothpick. Using the tip of the toothpick, tap drops of paint into the water. Swirl the paint in the water with the toothpick.

Try this...

Use two colours of paint to marbleize your paper. Simply tap two colours into the water. Swirl the paints with the toothpick. Then put your paper into the mixture and continue with Step 3.

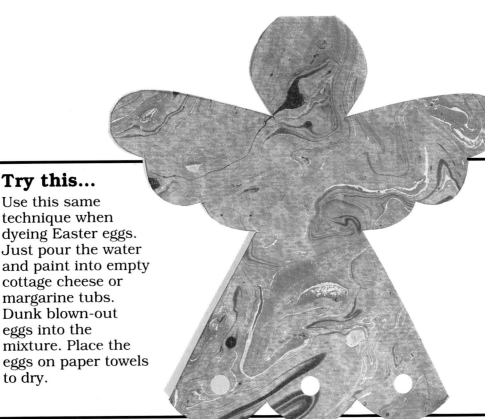

Try this...

Use this same technique when dyeing Easter eggs. Just pour the water and paint into empty cottage cheese or margarine tubs. Dunk blown-out eggs into the mixture. Place the eggs on paper towels to dry.

Make gift tags and holiday decorations...

Cut out patterns from unfolded sheets of paper to make gift tags and Christmas tree decorations. The star and the holly and angel gift tags in the photo on pages 10 and 11 are made this way.

3 Lay the paper on top of the water. With the tweezers or tongs, lift the paper from the water. Shake off the excess water. Prop the paper against the glass to dry.

Tap more paint into the water to marbleize another piece of paper. To change colours, swirl paper towels on top of the water. They will remove the paint. Then tap another paint colour on to the water.

4 Draw your own pattern or select a pattern of your choice from page 16. With the pencil, trace the pattern on to tracing paper. Cut out the tissue pattern. When the marbleized paper is dry, fold it in half. Lay the tissue pattern on top of the marbleized paper. Make sure the fold line of the pattern lies on top of the folded edge of the paper. Trace around the pattern. Cut out the design. Do not cut the folded edge. If you're making an angel, use the hole puncher to trim the bottom of her skirt. Write your Christmas greeting inside the card.

Ribbon Cards

Use scraps of gift-wrap ribbons to decorate
these easy-to-make cards.

Materials you will need...

☐ 22 x 30cm stiff
   coloured card

☐ Red, blue, yellow,
   and green gift-wrap
   ribbons

☐ 2cm gold star
   stickers

☐ Tracing paper

☐ Scissors

☐ Pencil

☐ Double-sided
   sticky tape or glue

☐ Rubber

Try this...

● Use other gift-wrap
ribbons and glue or
double-sided sticky
tape if you can't find
self-stick ribbons.

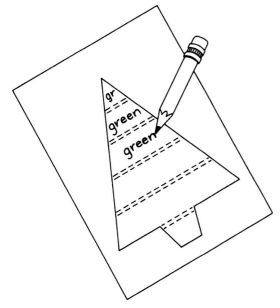

1 Select a pattern from page 17. Trace the
pattern on to tracing paper. Trace both
the solid and the broken lines. Write the
colour for each part of the pattern between
the broken lines. Cut out the pattern along
the *solid* line.

2 Fold the card in half. It should measure
11 x 15cm. Centre the pattern on top of
the folded card and use the pencil to lightly
draw around the shape.

3 Cut the tracing paper pattern apart
along the *broken* lines. The marked
tracing paper pieces will be used as
patterns to cut the ribbon.

4 Lay the patterns on the ribbons. Draw
around each shape. Cut out the shapes.

You can make Christmas tree decorations...

You can also use these card designs for Christmas tree decorations. Take an unfolded piece of stiff card or paper that is slightly larger than the pattern you want to make. Follow the instructions for making the cards, below. Then when the ribbon pieces are in place, cut around the design about 6mm from the ribbon edges. Punch a hole in the top of the ornament. String a 20cm piece of thread through the hole. Tie the thread ends in a knot to make a loop for hanging.

5 Stick some double-sided sticky tape or glue on to the back of each piece of ribbon and fasten it to the card within the drawn lines. When all pieces are in place, carefully rub out the pencil markings that remain. Add the gold star sticker to the top of the tree.

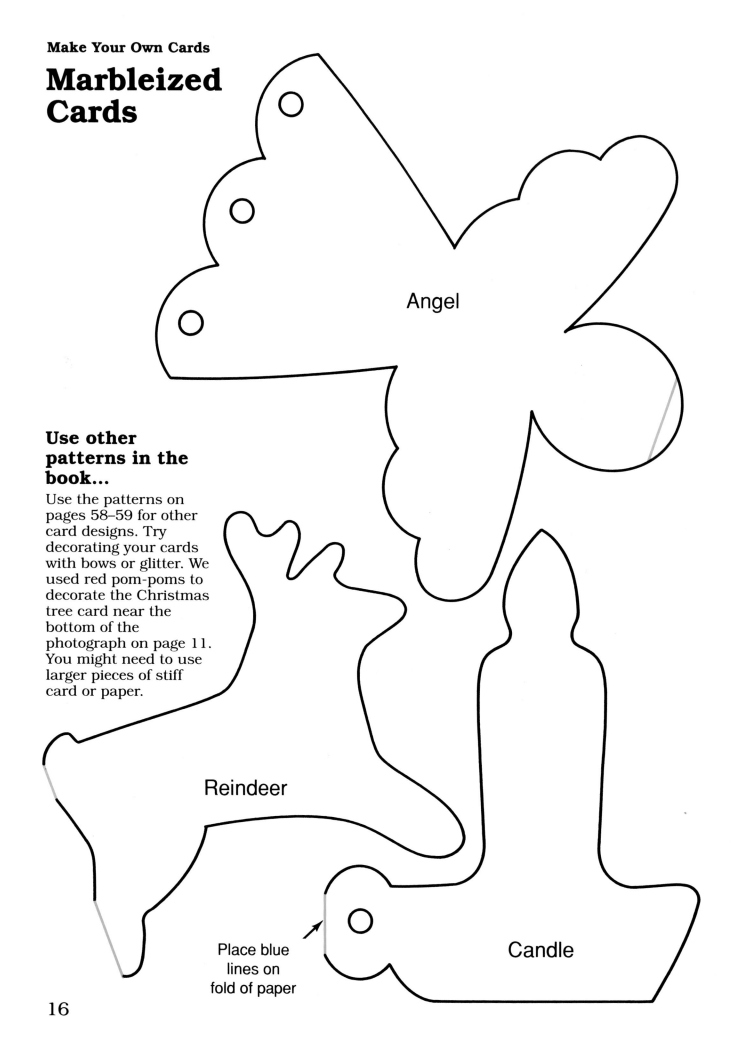

Marbleized Cards

Angel

Use other patterns in the book...

Use the patterns on pages 58–59 for other card designs. Try decorating your cards with bows or glitter. We used red pom-poms to decorate the Christmas tree card near the bottom of the photograph on page 11. You might need to use larger pieces of stiff card or paper.

Reindeer

Candle

Place blue lines on fold of paper

Ribbon Cards

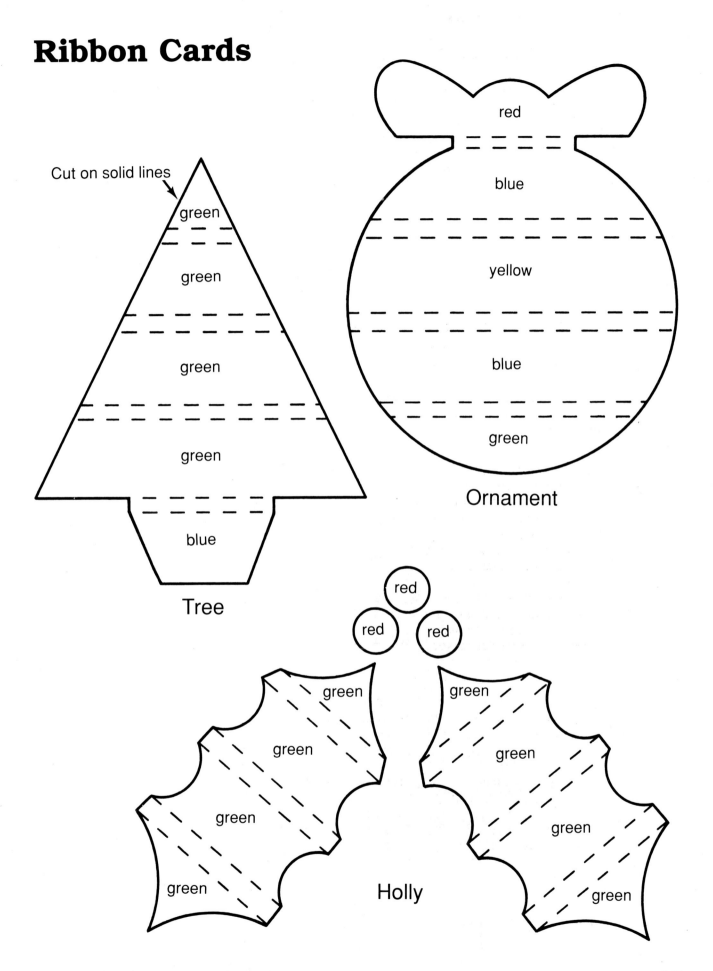

Cut on solid lines

green

green

green

green

blue

Tree

red

blue

yellow

blue

green

Ornament

red

red   red

green   green

green   green

green   green

green   green

Holly

Countdown To Christmas

Waiting for Christmas will be fun if you make this Advent calendar before the season starts. Then, starting on the first day of December, open one flap each day. When all the flaps are open, Christmas Day will have arrived!

Advent Calendar

Cut out some large and small evergreen trees from very stiff pieces of coloured card to begin your three-dimensional Advent calendar.

Materials you will need to make the trees...

- ☐ 16 sheets of very stiff 23 x 30cm green card
- ☐ Pencil
- ☐ Tracing paper
- ☐ Scissors
- ☐ Graphite or carbon paper

- ☐ Scalpel
- ☐ Scraps of coloured tissue papers
- ☐ 10 small stickers
- ☐ Sticky tape
- ☐ Green and blue wax crayons

- ☐ White glitter
- ☐ Pie dish
- ☐ Coins
- ☐ Glue stick
- ☐ Ruler

IMPORTANT

Ask a parent to cut the card with the scalpel. Do not try to use the scalpel yourself.

1 Use the pencil to trace the large-tree and small-tree patterns from pages 26 and 27 on to tracing paper. Cut out the patterns.

2 Place the patterns on the stiff green card and draw around them. Draw five large and five small trees. Cut out the trees. Use the graphite or carbon paper to trace the flaps and the broken lines on to the trees.

3 Ask a parent to cut the three slits for each flap using the scalpel and the ruler. Referring to the drawing above, cut along the solid lines. Do not cut along the broken line. Remember, the scalpel should only be used by a parent.

4 Gently push the flap away from you. Slide a piece of scrap paper *under* the tree but *over* the entire flap. Rub the four sides of the opening with the glue stick. Remove the scrap paper.

5 Fasten a square of coloured tissue paper to the opening. (The side with the tissue is the back of the tree.)

6 Turn the tree over. Carefully lift the flap (do not crease at this time). Fasten a sticker to the tissue paper.

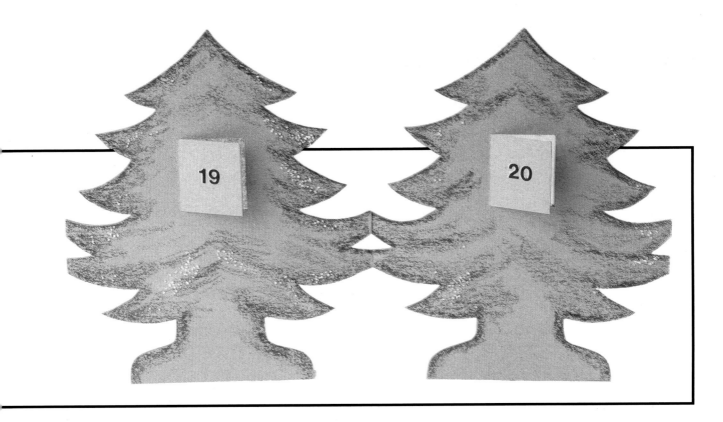

7 Use the green wax crayon to colour along the tree edges and to draw branches. Use the blue wax crayon to outline the tree and to highlight the branches.

8 Using the glue stick, spread glue over the coloured branches. Sprinkle glitter over the glue. With your fingers, push the glitter into the glue. Let the glue dry. Shake any extra glitter over the pie dish. Use this glitter on your next tree. Repeat steps 4–8 to make the remaining trees.

9 When all of your trees are completed, turn them over so the sides with the tissue paper are up. Tape the two widest branches of two large trees together. Cut away the tape that shows. Tape the three remaining large trees together in the same way. Repeat the same steps with first two, then three of the small trees.

10 Fold along the broken lines at the bottoms of the trees. To help the trees stand straight, place coins on the tabs.

Advent Calendar

Make this terrace house to add 12 more days
to your Advent calendar.

Materials you will need to make the terrace house...

- [ ] Two sheets of thick 23 x 30cm brown coloured card
- [ ] Glue stick
- [ ] Pencil
- [ ] Tracing paper
- [ ] Scissors

- [ ] Scraps of coloured tissue paper
- [ ] 12 small stickers
- [ ] Black ballpoint pen
- [ ] Coins
- [ ] Scraps of thick red coloured card

- [ ] Graphite or carbon paper
- [ ] Scalpel
- [ ] Ruler
- [ ] Black felt-tip pen
- [ ] Glue stick

**IMPORTANT
Ask a parent to
cut the card with
the scalpel. Do
not try to use
the scalpel
yourself.**

1 Use the pencil to trace the house pattern from page 28 on to tracing paper. Trace the roof, the door and window flaps, and tab lines. Do not cut out the pattern.

2 Lay the graphite or carbon paper between the thick brown coloured card and the tracing paper. Trace over the traced lines to transfer the pattern to the card. Trace all the house details, the window and door flaps, and the tab lines. Cut out the terrace house from the card.

The difference between graphite and carbon papers...

Both of these papers have a coated side that transfers markings from one sheet of paper to another. Graphite paper is heavier and easier to use. And, when you use graphite paper, you can rub out any mistakes you make as you trace your drawing. Both papers are available at crafts and art-supply stores.

3 Ask a parent to refer to Step 4 on page 20 to cut the window and door flaps. Remember, the scalpel should only be used by a parent.

4 Slip a piece of scrap paper under one of the window flaps. With the black felt-tip pen, outline the window flap. Repeat this step for all window and door flaps.

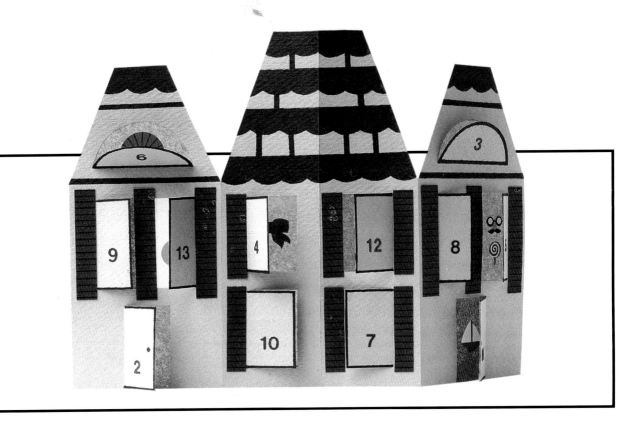

5 Colour the roof with the felt-tip pen. To avoid making smudges on your house, begin colouring in the centre of the house and work toward the edges.

6 Reverse the house so the front is facing downwards. Referring to steps 4 and 5 on page 20, fasten the tissue squares to the window and door openings. Reverse the house so the front is facing upwards. Fasten the stickers to the tissue squares.

7 With the black ballpoint pen, draw evenly spaced lines across the red card. Using the patterns on page 28, cut six large and six small shutters from this paper. Use the glue stick to fasten the shutters to the sides of the windows as shown in the photo, above.

8 Fold the house in half. Fold the tabs along the broken lines. Place coins on the tabs to keep the house from tipping over.

Advent Calendar

Complete your calendar by making these friendly snowmen,
a bright shining star, and some twig trees.

Materials you will need to make the snowmen, star, and trees...

- [ ] One sheet of 23 x 30cm thick white card
- [ ] Pencil
- [ ] Tracing paper
- [ ] Scissors
- [ ] Graphite or carbon paper
- [ ] Scalpel
- [ ] Ruler
- [ ] Glue stick
- [ ] Scraps of coloured tissue paper
- [ ] Three small stickers
- [ ] Scraps of thick orange, yellow, and black paper
- [ ] Black ballpoint pen
- [ ] Wooden skewer
- [ ] Sticky tape
- [ ] Bush twigs
- [ ] White paint
- [ ] Fruit pastels
- [ ] 6mm red vinyl or plastic adhesive numbers
- [ ] Hole puncher

IMPORTANT Ask a parent to cut the card with the scalpel. Do not try to use the scalpel yourself.

To make the snowmen...

1 Fold a piece of tracing paper in half. Place the fold of the tracing paper on the fold line of the snowman pattern on page 29. Use the pencil to trace the shape. Cut out the shape through both thicknesses of the paper. Do not cut along the fold. Unfold the pattern. Lay the pattern on top of the completed snowmen on page 29. Trace the eyes, mouths, and buttons of each snowman.

2 Lay the graphite or carbon paper between the thick white card and the snowmen pattern. Trace over the traced lines of the snowmen to transfer the pattern to the white paper.

3 Ask a parent to refer to Step 3 on page 20 to cut out the three sides of each flap. Remember, the scalpel should only be used by a parent.

4 Use the glue stick to fasten the tissue paper to the backs of the openings. Fasten the stickers to the tissue paper on the front side.

5 Trace the hat, scarf, nose, and arm patterns from page 29 on to tracing paper. Cut out these patterns.

6 Trace the scarf, hat, and arm patterns on to the black paper. Trace the nose pattern on to the orange paper. Cut out the shapes. Add carrot lines to the nose with the pen. Use the glue stick to fasten these pieces to the snowmen. Use the pen to draw mouths and colour eyes and buttons. (You can use a hole puncher to make large buttons.) Crease snowmen on fold line to stand.

To make the star...

1 Trace the star pattern from page 29 on to tracing paper. Cut out the shape.

2 Draw around the star shape on the white paper. Cut out the star.

3 **Ask an adult to refer to Step 3 on page 20 to cut out the three sides of the flap.**

4 Glue tissue paper to the back of the opening. Turn the star over and fasten a sticker to the tissue.

5 Cut five narrow strips of the yellow paper, each about 2cm long. Glue the strips to the back of the star.

6 Use sticky tape to fasten the back of the star to the top of the wooden skewer. Insert the other end of the skewer into a fruit pastel.

To make twig trees...

Paint the twigs with the white paint. When the twigs are dry, stand them in the fruit pastels.

To finish the calendar...

When you've completed all of the sections of your calendar, fasten the red adhesive numbers to each of the flaps. You will need enough stickers to make the numbers 1 to 25. Then, starting on the first day of December, fold back the flaps in their numbered sequence, one flap each day. Fold the flaps along the broken lines and make sharp creases to hold the flaps open.

Advent Calendar

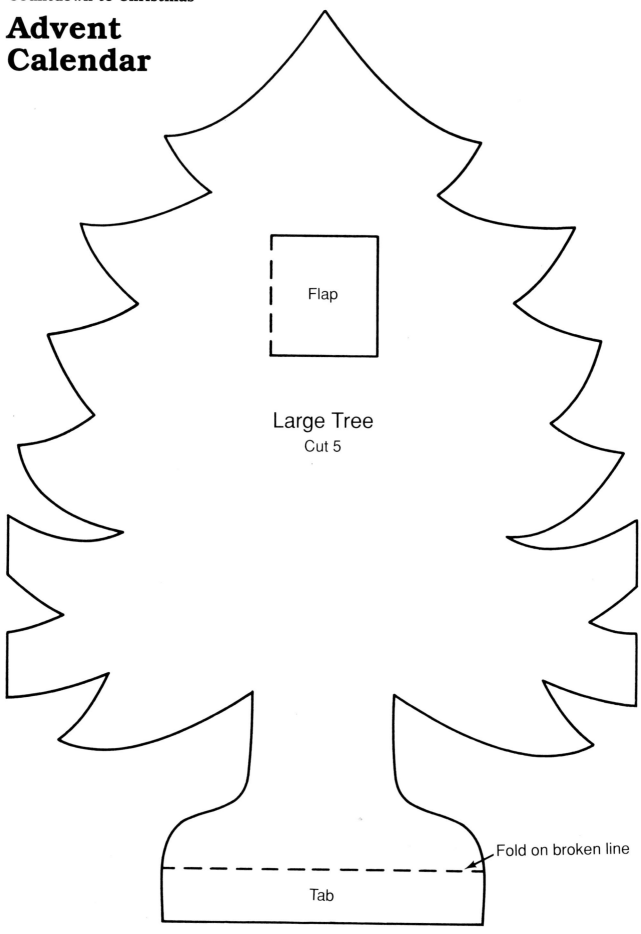

Flap

Large Tree
Cut 5

Fold on broken line

Tab

Use your school photos...

Use the small-tree pattern to make a card sure to be your grandparents' favourite. Begin by placing the pattern on a piece of thick card or paper. The straight edges of the two tree branches on the left side of the pattern should rest on the fold. Trace around the shape. Then cut out the tree and cut off the tab along the bottom edge. Do not cut along the tree edges that are on the fold.

Cut out an opening to fit the size of one of your school photographs. Glue the photo to the back side of the opening. Decorate your card as you wish and write a merry greeting inside.

Try this...

Instead of using stickers, cut small designs out of old Christmas cards or magazines and glue them to the tissue-paper squares on your Advent calendar. You might even write the numbers on the flaps with a red felt-tip pen instead of using the vinyl or plastic numbers. Go over the numbers several times with the pen so the numbers are clear.

Or, place these Advent calendar projects on the gingerbread-house landscape from pages 42 and 43. Just skip the terrace house and make 12 more trees or stars to take the place of the flaps on the house.

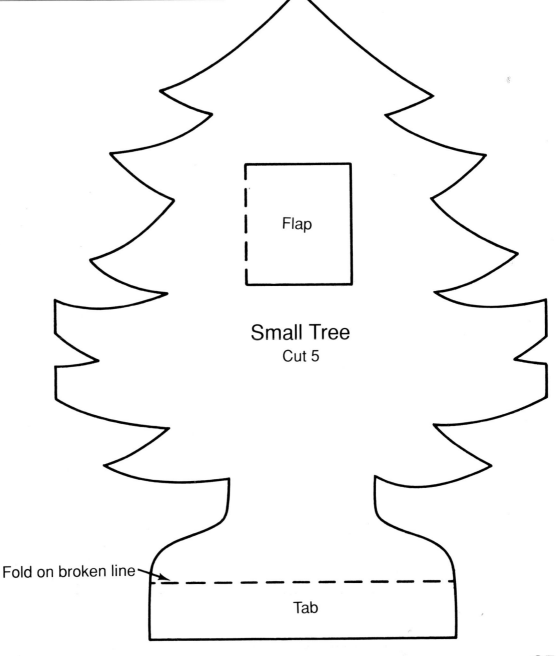

Flap

Small Tree
Cut 5

Fold on broken line

Tab

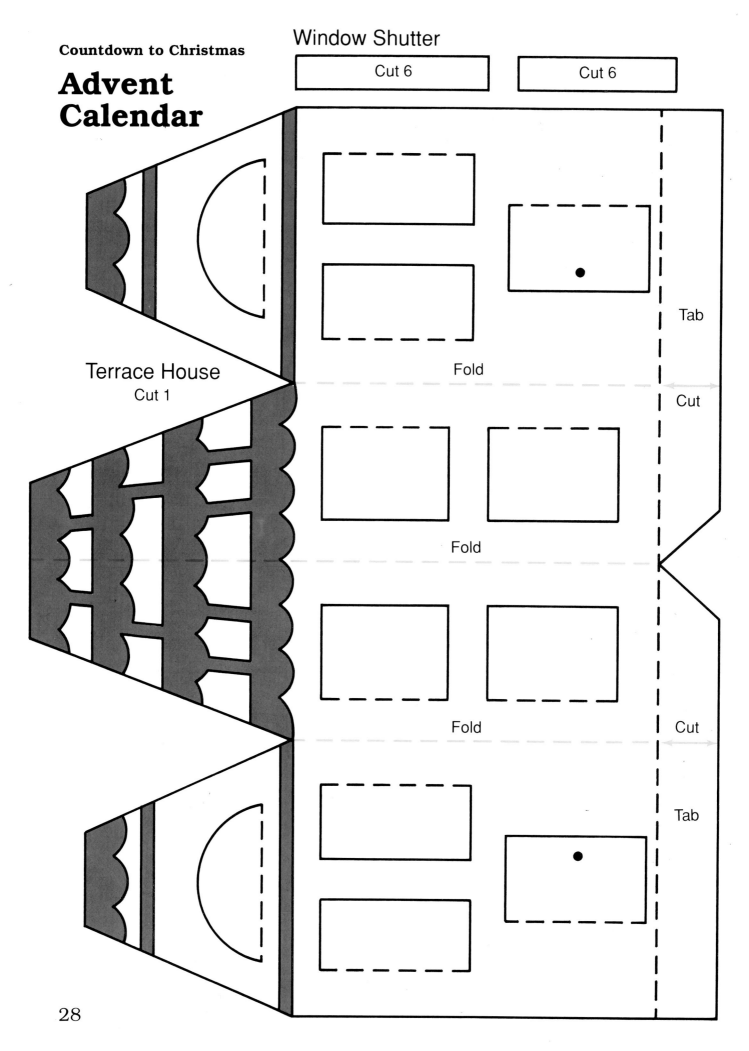

Countdown to Christmas

Advent Calendar

Window Shutter

Cut 6

Cut 6

Terrace House

Cut 1

Tab

Fold

Cut

Fold

Fold

Cut

Tab

28

Mr. Snowman   Mrs. Snowman

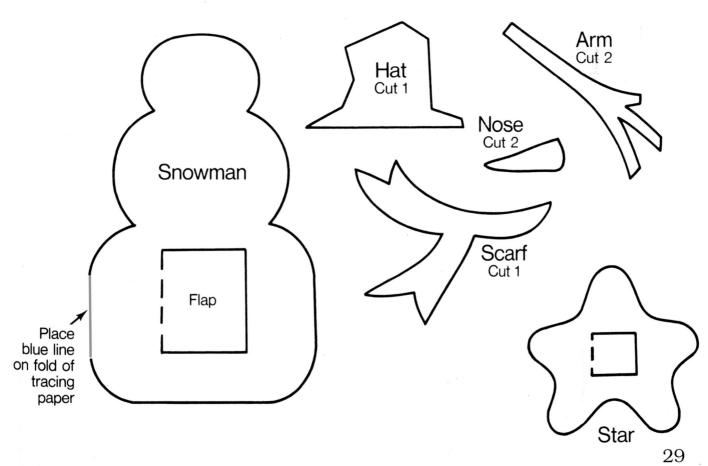

Snowman

Flap

Place
blue line
on fold of
tracing
paper

Hat
Cut 1

Arm
Cut 2

Nose
Cut 2

Scarf
Cut 1

Star

Gift-wrapping Presents

Tuck your Christmas presents into bags you make yourself. Use wallpaper scraps or other kinds of colourful papers. Then trim the bags with pinwheel bows, sticks of rock, or other decorations from this book.

Gift Bags

If you enjoy the Japanese art of paper folding, you'll love creating these bags to hide all of your gifts.

Materials you will need to make the middle-size bag...

- ☐ 28 x 48cm piece of wallpaper
- ☐ Ruler
- ☐ Pencil
- ☐ Glue stick
- ☐ Hole puncher
- ☐ Fancy string or ribbon
- ☐ Scissors
- ☐ Rubber

A

B

C

1 With the printed side of the wallpaper facing you, use the ruler and pencil to lightly draw a line down the centre of the paper. See Drawing A.

2 Again with the printed side facing you, fold one edge of the paper to the centreline. Fold the other edge so it overlaps the first edge by 2cm. Make sharp creases along the folds. See Drawing B.

3 Referring to Drawing C, use the ruler and pencil to draw a line 4cm in from each of the folds. With the scissors, cut 6mm slits through both thicknesses of the paper at the tops and bottoms of these drawn lines. You will make 4 small slits.

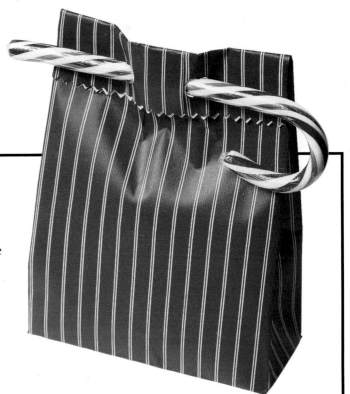

To make the small bag...

Use a 21 x 30cm piece of wallpaper. In Step 3, draw the lines and cut the slits 2cm in from the folds. In Step 6, draw the line 4cm from one of the narrow edges. Cut 4cm corner slits in Step 7.

To make the large bag...

Use a 35 x 50cm piece of wallpaper. In Step 3, draw the lines and cut the slits 5cm from the folds. In Step 6, draw the line 6cm from one of the narrow edges. Cut 6cm corner slits in Step 7.

D
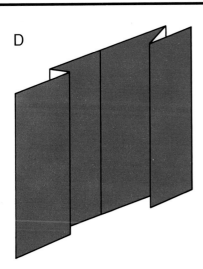

E
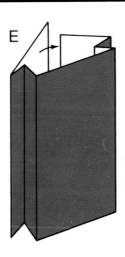

F
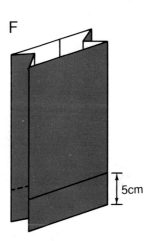

5cm

4 Using the slits as a guide and referring to Drawing D, fold back both flaps. Crease the folded edges.

5 Using the slits as a guide and referring to Drawing E, fold both flaps to the centre of the unprinted side of the wallpaper. Overlap the edges. Use the glue stick to fasten the edges. Rub out the pencil line on the printed side of the wallpaper.

6 To make the bottom of the bag, draw a line 5cm from one of the narrow edges. See Drawing F. Fold all thicknesses of the paper along this line and make a crease. Unfold, then fold and crease the paper in the other direction. Unfold, then run your hand through the inside of the bag.

Turn the page to finish the bags.

33

Gift Bags

continued

Use other ideas in this book to decorate your bags...

To add a festive touch to your gift bags, attach paper soldiers (the patterns are on page 8) coloured with felt-tip pens and decorated with sequins. Or tie paper-animal ornaments (the patterns are on page 40) to your bags. You can even slip a stick of rock or candy cane through the two punched holes to hold the bag closed, And for more paper-folding fun, decorate your bags with the pinwheel bows shown on the opposite page.

G

H

I

7 Using the folded lines you made in Step 6 on page 33 as a guide, cut 5cm slits in each of the four corners. See Drawing G.

8 Run the glue stick across one of the long edges at the bottom of the bag. Overlap the two long edges 1cm. Press them together. See Drawing H.

9 Referring to Drawing I, cut the short edges so they come to points in their centres. Rub the glue stick on the insides of these edges. Press these edges to the bottom of the bag.

10 Use the hole puncher to punch two holes through all thicknesses at the top of the bag. Thread with fancy string or ribbon. Tie in a bow. Trim the bag as you wish.

Pinwheel Bows

Decorate the bags with pinwheel bows made from Christmas wrapping papers.

Materials you will need...

- ☐ Scraps of wrapping papers
- ☐ Ruler
- ☐ Scissors
- ☐ Pencil
- ☐ Glue stick
- ☐ Coin

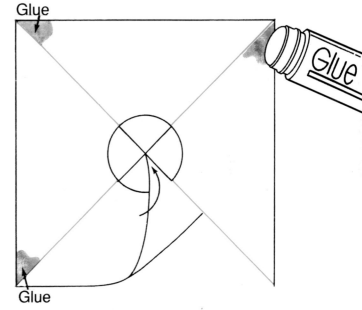

Glue

Glue

Glue

1 Rub the glue stick on the unprinted side of a square of wrapping paper. Glue this square to the unprinted side of a slightly larger piece of wrapping paper.

With the ruler and pencil, draw a square inside the smaller piece of paper. Draw two diagonal lines across the square to make one larger X. Cut out the square.

2 Lay the coin in the centre of the X where the two lines intersect. Draw around the coin. Using the blue lines in the drawing above as a guide, cut four diagonal lines.

3 Dab glue on to one of the two points at each slit. Bring one of these glued points to the centre and fasten it in place. Working around the square, continue to lift and take each glued point to the centre. With your finger, hold the points in the centre until the glue sets. Add more glue, if necessary.

To make large pinwheels, draw and cut 12cm squares. For small pinwheels, draw and cut 7 or 10cm squares.

35

Easy Decorations To Paint, Glue, Or Sew

To decorate and make the merriest of trees, make these enchanting animals from wallpaper scraps, and decorate vine wreaths with buttons and bows.

Paper-Animals

Wallpaper scraps and buttons are all you
need to make these playful animals.

Materials you will need...

- ☐ Print-wallpaper scraps
- ☐ Small (10mm-diameter) shirt buttons
- ☐ Embroidery wool or threads that match wallpaper colours
- ☐ Coloured felt-tip pens
- ☐ Thick green thread
- ☐ Scraps of felt (for bunny and bear scarves)
- ☐ Scraps of 6mm wide ribbon (for cat bow)
- ☐ Glue stick
- ☐ Sewing needle
- ☐ Scissors
- ☐ Tracing paper
- ☐ Soft-lead pencil

1 Select an animal pattern from page 40. Use a pencil to trace on to tracing paper the patterns for the body and the movable arms, legs, or tail. Trace the details of the face and the dots that mark the placement of the buttons. Cut out the patterns.

2 Cut the wallpaper scraps into 15cm squares. Using the glue stick, cover the back of one square of wallpaper with glue. Fasten the back of another wallpaper square to the first piece.

If you don't have scraps of wallpaper at your house, visit a D.I.Y. shop and ask about their out-of-date sample books. Most shops give away these books or only charge a small amount for them.

3 Trace the outlines of the animal patterns on to the wallpaper. Follow the directions on page 40 to determine the number of pieces to trace.

4 Referring to Step 1 on page 38, make your own carbon paper on the back of your tracing pattern. Use this carbon paper to transfer the face and all other markings to the wallpaper pieces.

5 With scissors, cut out the wallpaper shapes. Use the needle to punch holes through the dots on the shapes.

6 Thread the needle with double strands of thread that match the wallpaper. Knot the strands about 5cm from the end.

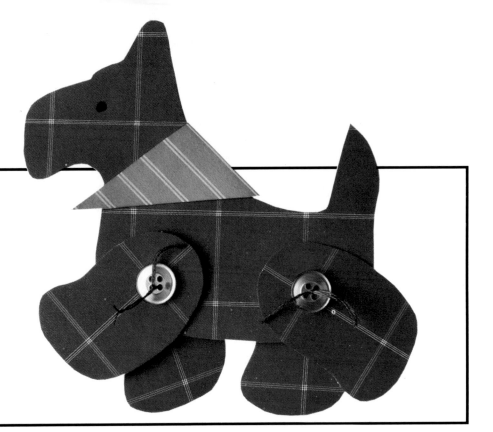

Try this...

For faster and easier assembly, use 1cm roundheaded fasteners to attach the arms and legs to the bodies.

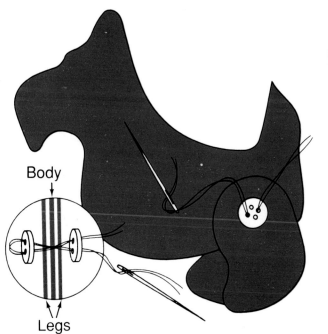

Body

Legs

7 Match the dots on *each* body part to the dots on the body. Using the directions that follow, sew one button to *each* side of the animal to attach the movable parts: Sew through the button, into the arm or leg, through the body, through the arm or leg on the other side, then through another button. Then push the threaded needle back through the body parts and the two buttons. Knot the ends of the thread. Trim the thread ends to leave 2cm strands. Repeat this step with the remaining body parts.

8 With the markers, draw the details of the face on both sides of the animal. Cut a scarf from a wallpaper scrap. Glue the scarf to the dog. Glue a ribbon bow to the cat and tie felt scarves to the bunny and bear.

9 Thread the needle with a 25cm piece of the thick thread. Draw the threaded needle through dot for the hanger. Remove the needle and knot the ends of the thread together to make a loop for hanging the paper animal.

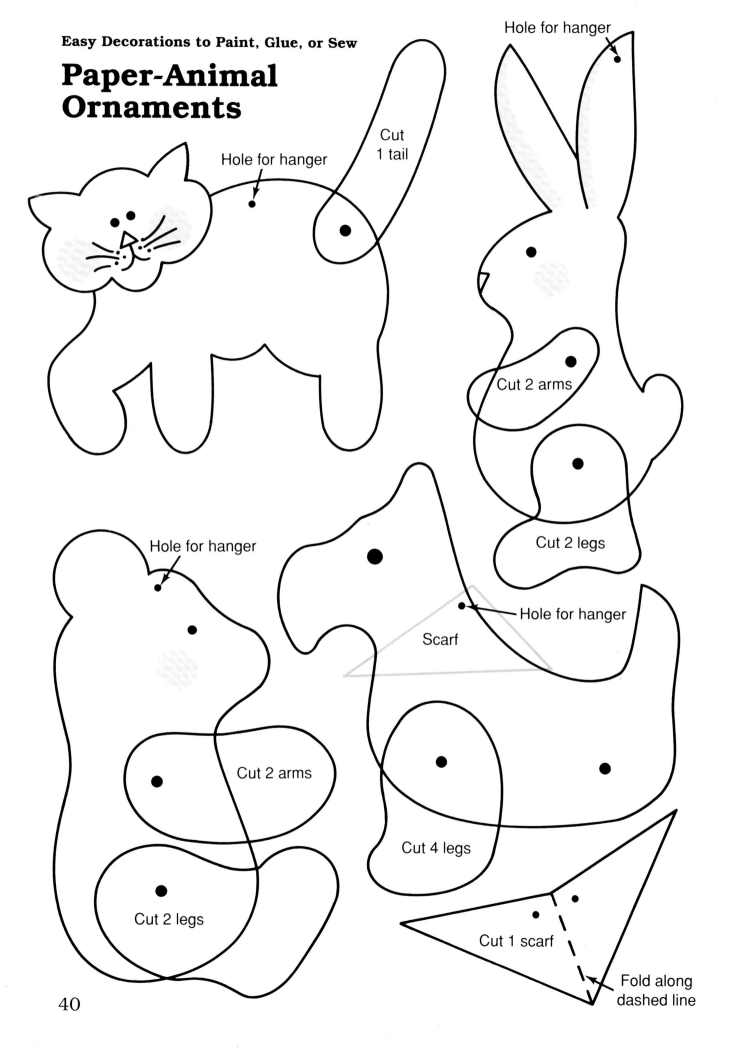

Easy Decorations to Paint, Glue, or Sew

Paper-Animal Ornaments

Hole for hanger

Cut 1 tail

Hole for hanger

Cut 2 arms

Cut 2 legs

Hole for hanger

Hole for hanger

Scarf

Cut 2 arms

Cut 4 legs

Cut 2 legs

Cut 1 scarf

Fold along dashed line

Vine-Wreaths

Glue colourful buttons and tie ribbon bows on tiny vine wreaths to trim your tree.

Materials you will need to make one wreath...

- ☐ Small (10cm) purchased vine wreath (available at most department stores)

- ☐ One metre each of 6mm-wide red and green ribbons

- ☐ Assorted shapes and sizes of red, green, and white buttons

- ☐ Glue

- ☐ Thick green thread

- ☐ Scissors

1 Put a dab of glue on the backs of the buttons. Fasten the buttons to the wreath, spacing them about 2cm apart. You can glue tiny white buttons on top of some or all of the red and green buttons.

2 Leaving a 17cm-long tail at the start, wrap the red ribbon around the wreath. Let the ribbon lie between the buttons as you wrap it. Then tie the ribbon ends.

3 Leaving a 17cm-long tail at the start, wrap green ribbon around the wreath in the opposite direction. Let the green ribbon overlap the red ribbon to form Xs between the buttons. Tie the green-ribbon ends.

4 Hold the ends of the red and green ribbons together and tie them into one bow. Loop a 28cm-long green thread around the top of the wreath. Knot the ends to make a loop for hanging.

Fun to Make Gingerbread House

Ask your family to help you make a gingerbread house that sits in a snowy scene. Gumdrops, sticks of rock or candy canes, chocolate bourbon biscuits, ice-cream cones, marshmallows, boiled sweets, and icing all combine to bring a cardboard house to life.

No-Bake Gingerbread House

Ask your parents or an older brother or sister to assemble the frame of your house from a cardboard box.

Materials you will need to assemble the house...

☐ Small cardboard box approximately 25 x 30cm and 45cm tall

☐ Pencil

☐ Ruler

☐ Scalpel

☐ Masking tape

IMPORTANT
Ask a parent to cut the box with the scalpel. Do not try to use the scalpel yourself.

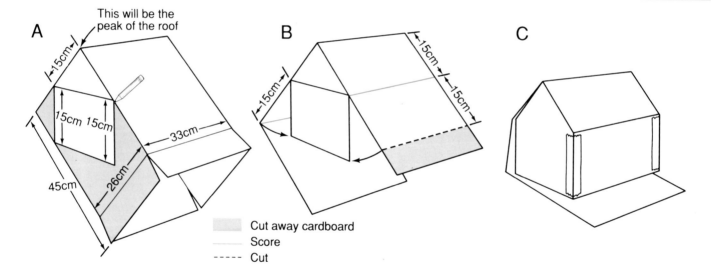

Cut away cardboard
———— Score
- - - - - Cut

1 **Note: The frame of the house should be built by a parent or an older teenager.** Standing at a table, place the box on one of its narrow sides so that the bottom faces away from you. Referring to Drawing A, mark 15cm from both sides of one corner on the side facing you. Draw a line to connect these two points. Then, from the two points, draw two 15cm lines perpendicular to the line you just drew. Draw a line to connect the ends of these two new lines.

Repeat this step on the opposite side of the box using the corresponding corner.

2 Ask a parent to use the scalpel to cut away the portion of the box that is shaded blue on Drawing A. Do the same on the opposite side of the box. The two narrow sides of the house and its roof peak are now established.

3 Referring to Drawing B, draw a straight line 15cm below, and parallel to, the roof peak on both of the long sides of the box. Use the scalpel to score these lines. Fold along the scored lines so that the long sides meet the narrow sides. Cut away the excess cardboard from the shorter of the two long sides to match the base of the house. Use the masking tape to fasten this long side to the two narrow sides.

Use other box sizes...

You can make frames for houses from all sizes of boxes following the directions below. For a larger box, use the same marking and cutting instructions. For a smaller box, change the 15cm markings and cutting instructions in steps 1 and 3 to 10 x 12cm dimensions. Adjust the door, window, and chimney measurements to conform to the new scale.

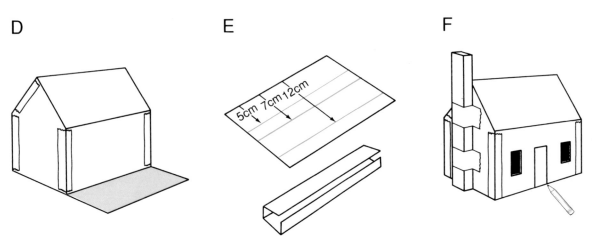

D

E

F

4 Referring to Drawing C, score the remaining long side along the base of the house. Fold along this score line and slide the cardboard under the house. Referring to Drawing D, tape the sides together and cut away the excess cardboard that extends from the base of the house. Tape the base edges.

5 To make the chimney, cut a piece of scrap cardboard to measure 15 x 33cm. Referring to Drawing E, draw lines 5cm then 7cm, then 12cm from one of the long edges of the strip. Score these lines. Fold the cardboard along the scored lines and tape the edges together. Tape the chimney to one of the house's narrow sides as shown in Drawing F.

6 Referring to Drawing F, cut two 4 x 6cm windows on each of the house's long sides. Mark one 4 x 10cm door on one of the long sides. Make sure the tops of the windows are in line with the top of the door.

Turn the page to decorate the house.

No-Bake Gingerbread House

You'll have lots of fun decorating your house
with colourful sweets and icing.

Materials you will need to decorate the house...

- ☐ Three batches of icing (see opposite page for recipe)
- ☐ Spatula
- ☐ Tube of white icing
- ☐ Vanilla-flavoured icing

- ☐ Cinnamon-covered chocolate bourbon biscuits
- ☐ Pink sugar wafers
- ☐ Pretzels
- ☐ 5 or 6 bags of assorted hard sweets

- ☐ Aluminium foil

1 Following the recipe opposite, make three batches of icing. Use the spatula to spread icing on one side of the house. Break the chocolate bourbon biscuits into sections. Cover the iced side of the house with the biscuit sections. Continue around the house, icing only one side at a time and covering the icing with the biscuit sections. Do not ice the triangular portions on the two narrow sides of the house at this time.

2 To make the shutters, decorate one side of eight pink wafers with the tube icing and small sweets. Fasten the shutters to the house. For the sills, fasten sweets to the bottoms of the windows.

For the door, use biscuit sections and a pink wafer cut in half. Decorate the two wafer pieces. Fasten the door pieces to the house. Outline the door with the tube icing. Add a sweet doorknob. Dip 15 pretzels into melted vanilla icing. Dry the pretzels on waxed paper. Fasten five pretzels above the windows and the door.

Recipe for one batch of icing...

3 egg whites, at room temperature
680g (24ozs) confectioners' sugar
½ teaspoon cream of tartar

Mix the egg whites, sugar, and cream of tartar in a small mixing bowl. Beat with an electric mixer on high speed until the icing is stiff. Add more sugar, if necessary. Cover the icing with a damp cloth and store in the refrigerator until you are ready to use it.

3 To make the overhangs on the long sides of the roof, fasten one row of biscuit sections along each roof edge. The biscuits should extend 1cm beyond the edges. Then ice one side of the roof. Working from the bottom, add rows of sweets to the roof. Then ice and decorate the other side of the roof.

Ice the two triangular portions on the narrow sides of the house. Cover with sweets. Fasten the remaining vanilla-iced pretzels along the bottom edges of the triangular sections.

4 Ice the chimney and decorate with sweets. Use the tube sweets to make the snow on top of the chimney. To make icicles, dribble short strips of tube icing on to foil and let dry. When dry, fasten the strips to the edges of the roof, the windowsills, and the chimney.

Decorate the bottom edges of the house with sweets. If you use gumdrops, cut them in half before you fasten them to the house.

Turn the page for instructions on how to decorate the landscape.

No-Bake Gingerbread House

Make a landscape from icing and other sweets to
create a winter wonderland for your gingerbread house.

Materials you will need to make the landscape...

- [ ] Three batches of icing (see recipe, page 47)
- [ ] Spatula
- [ ] Green and red paste food colouring

- [ ] Tube of white icing
- [ ] Twiglets
- [ ] Vanilla-flavoured icing
- [ ] Aluminium foil

- [ ] Large piece of cardboard
- [ ] Empty margarine tubs
- [ ] Masking tape
- [ ] Waxed paper
- [ ] Large marshmallows

- [ ] Ice-cream cones
- [ ] Small sweets
- [ ] Small sticks of rock
- [ ] Liquorice
- [ ] Toothpicks

1 Use the ice-cream cones to make the trees. First, colour two cups of icing with green food colouring. Cover the cones with the green icing. Then add small sweets to decorate the trees. When the icing on the trees is dry, dribble white icing on the treetops to look like snow.

To make taller trees, put a dab of icing on the tip of one cone and set a second cone on its top. Make lots of trees, but complete each one before going on to the next one. Set your trees on the iced cardboard base.

2 To make the fencing, first melt and colour two squares of the vanilla icing with red food colouring (to make it pink). Dip 30 twiglets into the pink icing. Lay the twiglets on waxed paper to dry.

To make one fence unit, run a string of tube icing down the middles of two coated twiglets. With their iced edges up, lay the two twiglets 2cm apart. Lay pink twiglets on top of the iced ones. Let the icing dry. Make three more fence units. Use tube icing to fasten the fences to the iced cardboard base.

To make a base...

Find a large piece of cardboard. Fasten upside-down empty margarine tubs to it with masking tape. Fasten aluminium foil to the cardboard to create a lake. Spread two batches of icing over the cardboard and tubs.

3 With the marshmallows, make shrubs to stand in front of the door. For best results, first leave the marshmallows out in the open for a couple of days. This makes their surfaces firmer and easier to work with. Poke a toothpick into one flat side of two firm marshmallows. Cover these two marshmallows with green icing. Decorate them with small sweets. Stick the ends of the toothpicks into undecorated marshmallows. Set the shrubs on the base.

4 For one sledge, use two small sticks of rock or candy canes and a piece of liquorice. Spread white icing along one side of the liquorice. Hold the two sticks of rock about 1cm apart and place the liquorice on top of the canes. Hold the sledge in place until the icing sets. Do not move the sledge until the icing dries. Repeat these steps to make more sledges. Set your sledges on the base.

Gifts for Santa

Why not leave Santa some gifts on a place mat and in a mug you've decorated just for him? He'll know you've been busy—and good—when he sees all the Christmas tree decorations and stockings you've made!

Felt Tree Decorations

Deck your tree with colourful felt tree decorations
to get Santa's attention on Christmas Eve.

Materials you will need...

- ☐ 23 x 30cm pieces of brown, red, white and black felt
- ☐ 5mm white pom-poms
- ☐ 7mm red pom-poms
- ☐ Glue stick
- ☐ Strong glue
- ☐ Tracing paper
- ☐ Pencil
- ☐ Hole puncher
- ☐ Needle
- ☐ Strong green thread
- ☐ Scissors
- ☐ Thin cardboard

1 Trace the outlines of the reindeer body and the antlers from page 58 on to tracing paper. Rub the glue stick over the back of the tracing paper. Fasten the tracing paper to the cardboard. Then cut out the pattern pieces.

2 Trace around the body pattern on to the brown felt. Trace around the antlers on to the white felt. Cut out the felt pieces. Use the hole puncher to punch out a black-felt eye.

Try this...

If you don't have red or white pom-poms, use the hole puncher to punch out the red-felt nose and the white-felt spots.

Add felt scarves...

The deer on Santa's place mat on page 50 have striped scarves. Use the pattern on page 58 to cut white felt scarves. Trim the scarves with strips of red felt. Glue the scarves to the deer's necks.

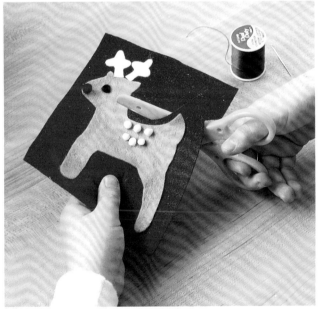

3 Cut an 11 x 15cm piece of red felt. Use the extra-sticky glue to fasten the body and antlers to the red felt. Make sure there is a narrow red border around *all* sides of the deer. Glue a red pom-pom in place for the nose. Glue the eye in place. Then glue five or six white poms-poms to the deer's back.

4 When the glue is dry, cut the deer from the red felt. Leave a narrow red border to outline the deer's shape. Thread a needle with a 30cm length of thick thread. Pull the thread through the top of the ornament. Knot the ends of the thread to make a loop for hanging the ornament. Repeat steps 1–4 to make additional ornaments.

On pages 58–59 you'll find patterns for other felt ornaments.

Christmas Stockings

Santa will get a kick out of this stocking that
you can make all by yourself.

Materials you will need...

- ☐ 45cm of red-and-white checked flannel-backed vinyl
- ☐ 2cm self-adhesive red vinyl or plastic letters
- ☐ 7mm-diameter green macramé cord

- ☐ Dressmaker's pins
- ☐ Scissors
- ☐ Pencil
- ☐ Tracing paper
- ☐ Glue stick

- ☐ Large piece of brown paper or brown paper bag
- ☐ Strong glue
- ☐ Hole puncher
- ☐ Sticky tape

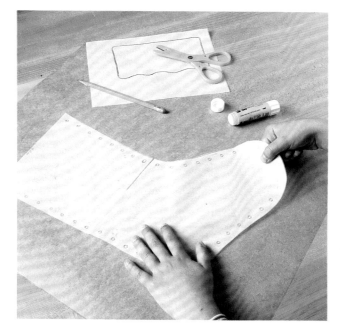

1 Trace the stocking patterns (foot and top) from pages 60–61 on to the tracing paper. Trace the lacing holes. Cut out the patterns. Cut the paper bag to make one large piece of paper. Rub the glue stick over the backs of the traced patterns. Fasten the patterns to the brown paper to make one stocking pattern. Cut out the pattern from the brown paper. Trace the cuff pattern from page 61 on to the tracing paper. Cut out the pattern.

2 Fold the checked vinyl in half with the flannel sides facing. Pin the stocking pattern to the vinyl. Cutting through the two thicknesses of the vinyl, cut out the stocking. Do not remove the pattern from one vinyl. Pin the cuff pattern to one thickness of the vinyl. Cut out the cuff.

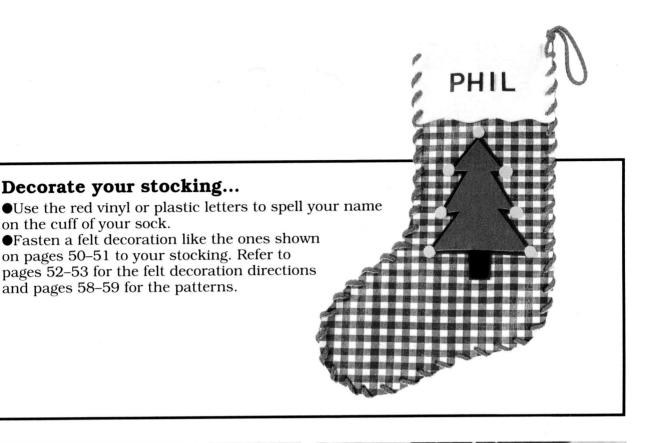

Decorate your stocking...

● Use the red vinyl or plastic letters to spell your name on the cuff of your sock.

● Fasten a felt decoration like the ones shown on pages 50–51 to your stocking. Refer to pages 52–53 for the felt decoration directions and pages 58–59 for the patterns.

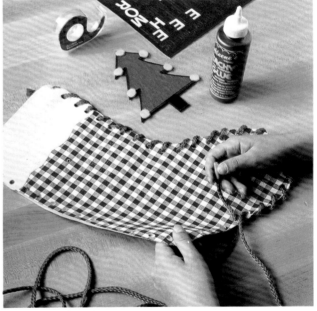

3 Use the hole puncher to punch out the lacing holes around the stocking. Punch through both the pattern and the two thicknesses of the vinyl. When all the holes are punched, remove the pattern.

4 Put several dabs of the strong glue in the centre of the vinyl side of the cuff. Fasten the cuff to one side of the stocking. This is the front. When the glue is dry, turn the stocking so its back is up. Punch holes through the cuff using the holes that are already punched as guides.

5 Cut a 2m length of macramé cord. Knot one end of the cord. Wrap the other end with tape. From the back of the sock, push the taped end through the top lacing hole on the *toe* side of the sock. Pull the cord until the knot rests against the lacing hole. Take the cord to the back of the sock and thread it through the next hole. Lace the sock in this manner. When the lacing is complete, knot the cord to make a loop for hanging. Slip the remaining cord under two inches of the lacings on the back. Cut the excess cord. Glue the cord end to the sock.

Santa's Place Mat and Mug

Use the reindeer or any of the other felt tree decorations
to decorate a place mat and mug for Santa's snacks.

Materials you will need...

- [ ] Hole puncher
- [ ] 35 x 50cm piece of red-and-white-checked flannel-backed vinyl
- [ ] Masking tape
- [ ] Sticky tape
- [ ] Scissors
- [ ] 3m of 6mm-diameter green macramé cord
- [ ] 76cm of 3mm-diameter green macramé cord
- [ ] Pencil
- [ ] Strong glue
- [ ] Scraps of red and white felt
- [ ] Tracing paper
- [ ] Purchased mug

To make the place mat...

1 Place the checked vinyl piece so the vinyl side is up. Fold under each of the four sides about 2cm. Crease the folds. Place small pieces of masking tape on the flannel side to temporarily hold the folds in place.

2 Use the hole puncher to punch holes through both thicknesses of the vinyl. Space the holes 2cm apart and 6mm away from the folds.

3 Knot one end of the 6mm-diameter macramé cord. Tape the other end with a strip of sticky tape (to look like the end of a shoelace).

4 From the flannel side of the mat, push the taped end of the cord through one of the lacing holes. Pull the cord until the knot rests against the hole. Take the cord to the flannel side of the mat and thread it through the next lacing hole. Continue to lace the mat in this manner. When the lacing is completed, slip the end of the cord under 51mm of the lacings on the flannel side of the mat. Trim the excess cord. Glue the end of the cord to the mat.

5 To decorate the mat as shown opposite, make three reindeer ornaments following the directions on pages 52–53. Referring to the photograph on the opposite page, glue the deer to the vinyl side of the mat. Use the 3mm-diameter cord to make the reins as follows: Glue one end under the scarf of the reindeer on the left side. Drape the cord to the centre deer, and then to the last deer. Glue the cord under each scarf. Take the remaining cord to the back side through a lacing hole. Trim the excess cord. Glue the end of the cord to the mat.

To make the mug...

1 Trace the cane heart in the drawing on the right on to tracing paper. Cut out the pattern.

2 Draw around the pattern on to the white felt. Draw two cane shapes. Cut out the shapes. Glue narrow strips of red felt on top of the white felt to create the striping.

3 Using the drawing on the right as a guide, glue the canes to a piece of red felt. When the glue is dry, cut the shape from the red felt. Leave a narrow red border to outline the shape. Glue the decoration on one side of the mug. Using a 20cm piece of macramé cord or ribbon, tie a bow round the handle, as in the picture above.

Mug Pattern

Felt Tree Decorations

Glue the decorations to a piece of felt (you choose the colour) as shown in Step 3 on page 53. Then cut around the ornaments as shown in Step 4.

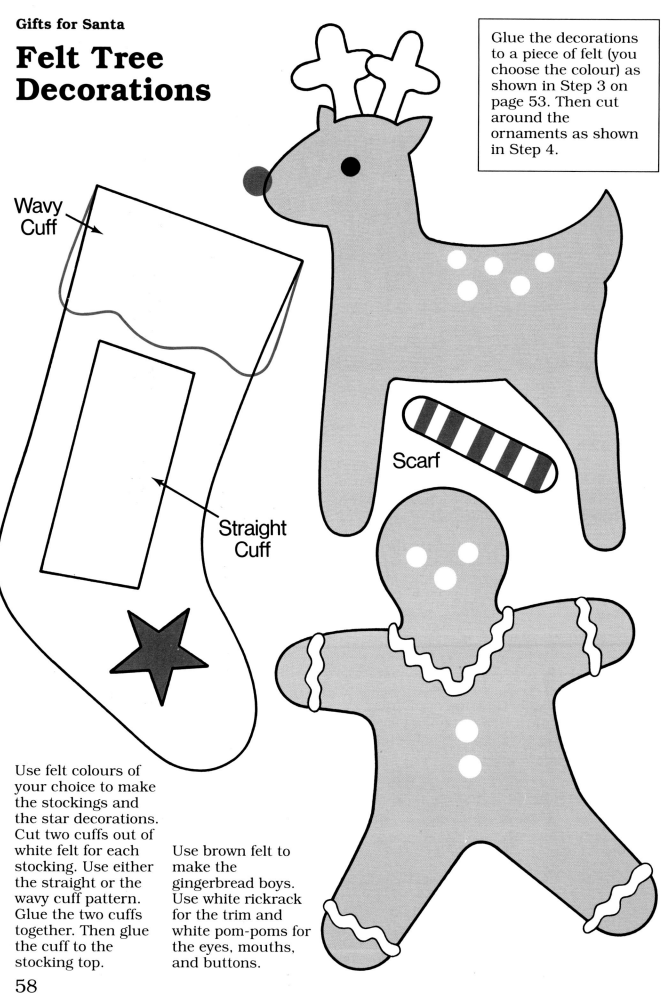

Wavy Cuff

Straight Cuff

Scarf

Use felt colours of your choice to make the stockings and the star decorations. Cut two cuffs out of white felt for each stocking. Use either the straight or the wavy cuff pattern. Glue the two cuffs together. Then glue the cuff to the stocking top.

Use brown felt to make the gingerbread boys. Use white rickrack for the trim and white pom-poms for the eyes, mouths, and buttons.

Use green felt to make the trees and black felt to make the trunks. Glue red pom-poms to the branches after the trees have been cut from the felt backing pieces.

Use brown felt for the lollipop sticks. Use a felt colour of your choice for each lollipop circle. Cut the swirl from the white felt and glue it to the lollipop circle.

Use felt colours of your choice to make the stars.

Use white felt to make the canes. Then, for the stripes, glue narrow strips of red felt to the white felt.

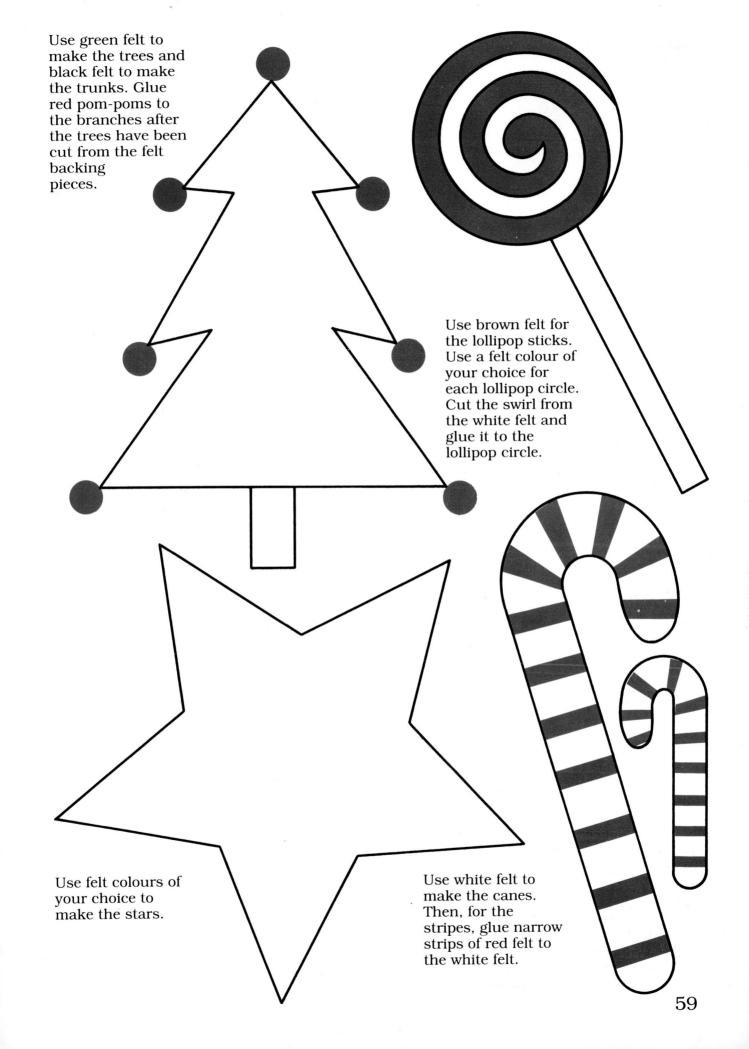

Christmas Stockings

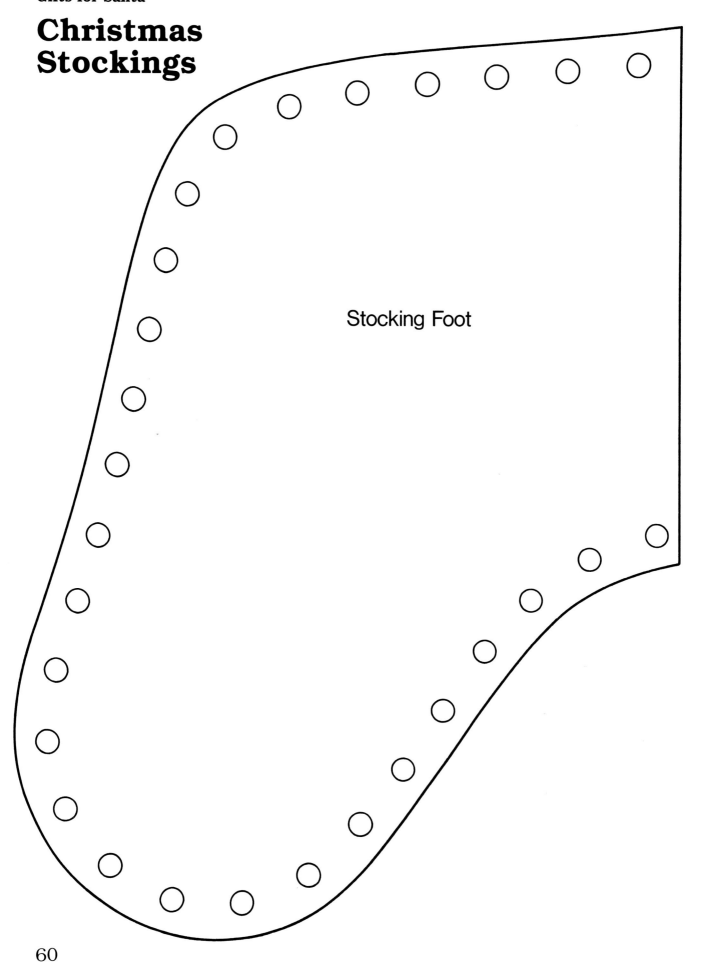

Stocking Foot

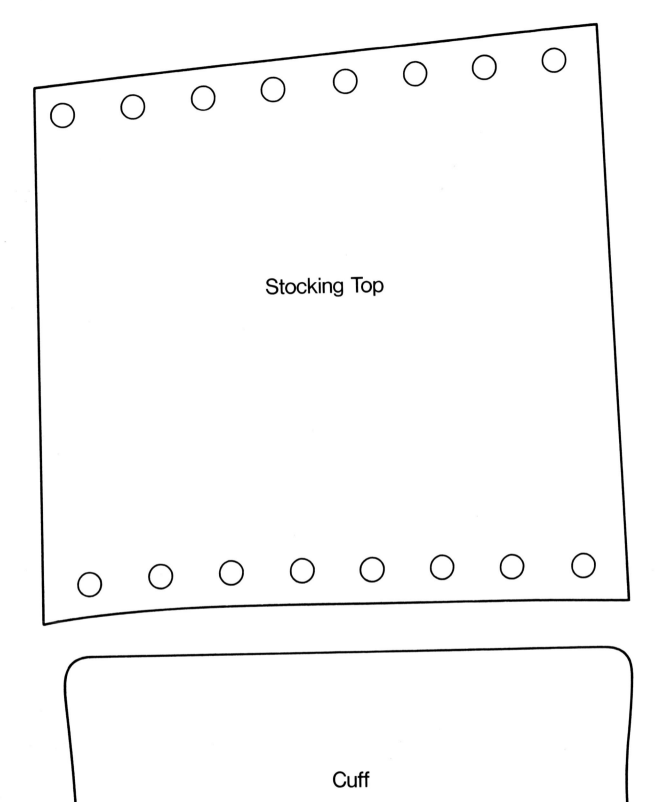

Stocking Top

Cuff

ACKNOWLEDGEMENTS

We are pleased to acknowledge the photographer whose talents and technical skills contributed much to this book.

Hopkins Associates

For their co-operation and courtesy, we extend a special thanks to the following sources.

Hallmark Cards, Inc.
Kansas City, MO 64141

Papercraft Corp.
Papercraft Park
Pittsburgh, PA 15238